SERMON OUTLINES ON

the Gospels

By Mark Scott

Standard Sermon Starters

Sam E. Stone, Editor

STANDARD
PUBLISHING
Cincinnati, Ohio

To maintain the brevity and usefulness of these outlines for
preaching, information about all sources cited can be found on
page 63 rather than in the text itself.

The Standard Publishing Company, Cincinnati, Ohio
A division of Standex International Corporation

© 1995 by The Standard Publishing Company
All rights reserved
Printed in the United States of America

01 00 99 98 97 96 95   5 4 3 2 1

Library of Congress Cataloging-in-Publication Data

Scott, Mark, 1953-
    Sermon outlines on the Gospels / Mark Scott.
        p.   cm.
    Includes bibliographical references (p.)
    ISBN 0-7847-0402-3
    1. Bible. N. T. Gospels—Sermons—Outlines, syllabi, etc.
I. Title.
BS2555.4.S36   1995
251'.02—dc20   95-16198
                                              CIP

To four preachers:

To my father, Robert A. Scott,
under whose preaching I became a Christian.

To Don DeWelt,
who made me "want to preach."

To Wayne Shaw,
*who taught me and who continues
to teach me "how to preach."*

To J. K. Jones
*My favorite preacher who labors with me
in the yoke of training preachers.*

Table of Contents

Introduction

What Preaching from the Gospels Should Be

"I must preach . . . because that is why I was sent" (Luke 4:43). Jesus
Christ was a preacher! And, He was a good one. He spoke with authority
(Matthew 7:29), the crowd listened to him with delight (Mark 12:37),
and the people hung on His every word (Luke 19:48). Not only was Jesus
a preacher, but Matthew, Mark, Luke, and John were as well.

A preacher who studies the Gospels to "find a sermon" quickly realizes that someone else has already preached this material. Before any of it
was written down and became part of the canon it was given orally.
Therefore it already has a shape that the Bible preacher wants to respect.
This is not one's first impression however because the material has been
"polished" by the inspired Gospel writer. When preachers speak it is for
presentation. When preachers write it is often for publication. Thus,
when someone reads the Gospels they might not assume that they are
reading some of the early sermonic material of Jesus and the early church,
but they should. For all the Gospels are, to some extent at least, intended
to be sermonic.

What then should preaching from the Gospels be? First it should be
Christ-centered. All the Gospels are unsigned. The writers go out of their
way to hide off-stage. The lead is played by the Son of God. Those interested in preaching biographical sermons from the Gospels should remind
themselves that Jesus is the hero of all the narratives. The spotlight is
clearly on Him. And, modern critics should remind themselves that only
Jesus saves—not Matthew, Mark, Luke, nor John. Some, for instance, are
more interested in what the Gospels tell us about Matthew's church than
they are in simply reading about the words and deeds of Jesus. This
would clearly embarrass the inspired evangelists.

Second, it should be redemptive and evangelistic. The words and
deeds of Jesus are powerful to transform the listener. They need to be
preached with that power. People to whom the Gospels are preached
should flee from the wrath to come and run into the arms of Jesus. He
and He only can save to the uttermost.

Third, it should be revealing of the author's intent and slant. This is
not to contradict what was said earlier. Only Jesus saves. But the Gospel
writers did have stock in that which they recorded by the inspiration of
the Holy Spirit. The Gospels are very much alike, but they are also very

different. Their portraits of Jesus differ. Preaching from the Gospels should pick up on those different brush strokes. Matthew presents the compassionate and authoritative king who will fulfill God's plan to the nations. Mark presents the busy and powerful Son of God who serves the needs of man. Luke presents the cosmic Christ who will meet the needs of all mankind by including all the outsiders in God's grace. And John presents the divine Word from God as indicated by signs and sermons.

Fourth, it should be based squarely on a specific text. This is not to suggest that one cannot preach well in a topical fashion from the Gospels. Indeed the parallel passages should at least be considered as there are often many of them. However a Gospel text, kept within its literary context, which records one event, encounter, and sermon from Jesus will probably be most portable for the contemporary audience. While change of event in the Gospels does not always mean change of theme, each text has some hermeneutical integrity, and that should be respected.

Fifth, it should be indicative of the wide variety of Gospel genre. Preaching from the Gospels should never run the preacher into a rut. Built into the material is a vast array of types of literature. We find narratives, encounters and dialogues, parables, miracles, genealogies, and prophecies to mention only a few. When preaching from the Gospels the sermons should not all sound the same.

Sixth, it should have the accent on good news. The post-modern world has produced a western culture filled with despair and lacking in significance. To boomers who are attempting to find their way back to the church and to busters who have found that their center has collapsed, preaching from the Gospels has the greatest prospect of positive good news. They are, after all, Gospels.

This book of sermons is an attempt in the direction of variety. I have attempted to share sermons from all four Gospels, from a variety of genre, from a variety of textual lengths, from a variety of themes, and from a variety of occasions that would match some of the special Christian seasons. For the most part the sermons follow a basic chronological flow from a harmonized study of the life of Christ. May those who have ears to hear, hear.

The Best of the Good News

John 3:16, 17

Introduction

I like familiar things! My motto is, "Consistency, thou art a jewel." Launching out into the deep of unfamiliar territory is not my idea of a good time.

Therefore, what could be more harmless than looking at the golden text of the Bible? But be careful—Fred Craddock reminds us that after the "nod of recognition" comes the "shock of recognition." Are there new truths to learn from old familiar places? The best of good news is that:

I. The Good News Is Cosmic in Scope.

A. Consider the use of "everyone" (v. 15) and "whoever" (v. 16).

B. Consider that "world" appears four times in verses 16-17.

C. Consider the encounters that Jesus had in these first chapters in this Gospel. The gospel is wide enough to include:
    1. A religious leader (chapter 3).
    2. A morally-wounded woman (chapter 4).
    3. A Roman official (chapter 4).
    4. A lame man (chapter 5).
    5. A host of hungry people (chapter 6).
    6. An array of enemies (chapters 7, 8, and 10).
    7. A blind man (chapter 9).
    8. A family in grieving (chapter 11).

II. The Good News Is Warm in Appeal.

A. The warmth is seen in God's love (v. 16) and God's heart (v. 17). He doesn't want to condemn the world.

B. But the warmth is not sticky and mere sentiment. The verses that surround the golden text of Scripture deal with the wrath of God (v. 18-20). Maybe this is the only way to appreciate the love of God—i.e. see it against the backdrop of His justice.

C. This warmth must be retained as we share the message. Let us not only win the war of argumentation but also the battle of presentation. For how we share the message is almost as important as what we share. Augustine said, "God loves each one of us as if there was only one of us to love. "

III. The Good News Is Available Through Belief.

A. Belief is a key term in John's Gospel (cf. 20:30-31). It is used numerous times and always—with one exception—as a verb. From John's perspective, belief is something one does.

B. Belief is simple and profound at the same time. It astounds the scholar, but the little children can understand.

C. Belief, in the final understanding, is the commitment of one's life to Christ in unconditional loyalty.

IV. The Good News Is Eternal in Life.

A. Life is also a key term in John's Gospel (cf. 20:30-31).

B. Life is viewed from two perspectives in John:
 1. In terms of quality (10:10b). This is life lived at the highest level.
 2. In terms of duration (5:24). God's glorious future has invaded our present through the Christ-event.

C. Life is not the accumulation of stuff nor the storing up of things. That which was forfeited in the garden is regained through Christ.

Conclusion

No doubt this all sounded astounding to Nicodemus (cf. v. 4, 10). But he would later appreciate its truthfulness (19:39).

Perhaps that's how it sounds to post-modern man. The only objection might be that it is too good to be true.

A Welcome Visit

Luke 1:67-79

Introduction

Some visitors are rather intrusive. They are like your relatives at Christmas who remind you of Proverbs 25:17, "Seldom set foot in your neighbor's house—too much of you, and he will hate you. "

Other visitors are tolerated. You don't enjoy them much, but you can get through it with God's help. And, you usually feel good that you endured it. It's something like kissing your sister.

But some visitors refresh you. They are very welcome, and you come away as a better person. You are glad to roll out the red carpet for them because they stimulate you and leave you never the same.

When Jesus visited earth his visit was received in all three of these ways. Zechariah was never the same as a result of the Son of God's visit. You remember the plot: Luke's orderly account begins with a priest's encounter with an angel. The encounter left him silent until his son was born. When he was able to speak his first words they were about God's visit to earth. Only later did he talk about his own son.

In the coming of Jesus Christ, God visited the world and left it never the same. For that visit, from Zechariah's perspective, was:

I. A Spiritual Visit.

A. The language is political: horn, David's reign, deliverance from enemies, preparation for a king's visit, and peace.

B. But the meaning of the language is spiritual: redemption, salvation, forgiveness, mercy, remembered covenant, service to God, and light for those in darkness.

II. A Long-Awaited Visit.

A. One thing that makes Christmas to be Christmas is the sense of anticipation. Only Easter could rival that sense of the giving of new life.

B. In a sense this is the last prophecy before the coming of the Messiah. We should notice the longing that is in it. It is similar to Simeon's response (Luke 2:28-32).

III. An Effectual Visit.

A. Some visits happen and leave you with a first-class yawn—the paper boy, the mail man, the meter man.

B. But this visit makes an actual difference. John the Baptist's whole life is wrapped up in this prophecy. Our service, holiness, righteousness, moral excellence, and peace are at stake.

Conclusion

Jesus got upset because the Jews didn't recognize their visitor (Luke 19:44). There are few things as embarrassing as being in the presence of greatness and not knowing it. Will Christmas catch us unaware of what God is doing in the world?

Will you respond like scrooge, complaining about this visit? Will you respond like the Jews, nonchalant? Or will you respond like Zechariah, in salvic song?

Illustrations

Asleep on Greatness. Some years ago I was preparing to take my place by my wife's side at the Missouri Christian Convention. While attempting to get out of the aisle and be seated I bumped into a handsome looking man. He excused himself, and I said, "Excuse me." He then stuck out his hand and said, "My name's John Ashcroft. What's yours?" I said, "I'm Mark Scott—nice to meet you John." He proceeded down the isle, and I got seated for the evening session. I thought to myself, "John Ashcroft, John Ashcroft, I should know that name from somewhere." Then to my horror, I watched as the honorable governor of the state of Missouri, John Ashcroft, took the stage to greet the convention audience. I could have died. I was sure that I had egg all over my face. How much worse to be visited by the God of the universe and not know it.

Agenda on something other than the real purpose for his coming. Some years ago I read about a legend that surrounded a Christmas party thrown by Satan. He was quoted as saying to his demons, "Keep everyone very merry, very merry indeed. If they ever take this story about God visiting earth seriously we'll really be in trouble."

The Insignificant in Christmas

Luke 2:1-20

Introduction

The Christmas story has everything needed for a great story: Political intrigue, conflict, anticipation, the drama of a delivery room, fear, doxology, and amazement.

But one thing that impresses about the Christmas story is how simple and unadorned it really is. In fact what captures me is the "insignificant" element.

Some might object by saying, "Insignificant?" How could the birth of the virgin-born Son of God be insignificant? Indeed for God to become human (John. 1 :14) is no small thing. But watch how the only Gentile (outsider) to write a life of Christ shows in the Christmas story how God fills the seeming insignificant with His presence and makes what might have been mundane into profound mystery.

I. Insignificant Places.

A. The "happening" places of the world were Rome and Syria. People who ruled others lived there, and that mattered. No one cared much about Palestine, tucked away in a small pocket of the Roman Lake (Mediterranean Sea)—except God.

B. But our story sets its focus on little places:
    1   Like Bethlehem—granted, the City of David, but really not all that important in terms of size and clout.
    2. Like Nazareth—and even Nathanael asked, "Can anything good come out of Nazareth?" (John 1:46).
    3. Like a manger—a common cow trough but mentioned three times in our text.
    4. Like fields—where shepherds watch flocks. The first Christmas took place "down on the farm."

C. When God comes near all the little places become big!

II. Insignificant People.

A. The important people of the world were mentioned in v. 1 & 2: Caesar Augustus and Quirinius. They were the movers and shakers. When they spoke people listened. They could call for taxes and the word was, "So let it be done."

13

B. But our story looks to different key players:
   1. Like a young poor couple from Nazareth—Mary and Joseph.
   2. Like shepherds—Biblically shepherds had important roles, but socially they were outcasts.
   3. Like the innkeeper—this person is so insignificant that technically he is not even mentioned in the text.

C. When God comes near all the little people suddenly seem to matter!

III. Insignificant Event.

A. The event that would makes news was taxes—it still does.

B. But our story gives attention to the birth of a baby. Granted, for the believer this is anything but normal:
   1. There was the matter of fulfilled prophecy.
   2. There was the matter of the appearance of that star.
   3. There was the matter of the virgin conception and birth.

C. But think: God started to save the world with the birth of a baby. Babies are born everyday. The Bethlehem paper would have read the next morning: Joseph and Mary, a boy. Big deal—it happens every day. But therein is the wisdom of God (cf. 1 Corinthians 1:26f). When God comes near all little events take on spiritual power!

Conclusion

For the Gospel written for the outsider this was very good news. Christmas announces that all places, all people, and all events matter to God.

Hebrews says that He had "to share in their humanity" (Hebrews 2:14). This He did, so at least all could relate to this Cosmic Christ. Had He come in royalty only the rich could have appreciated Him. He is truly a man for all seasons!

Clouds at Christmas
Matthew 2:13-23

Introduction

It would surprise no one to say that Christmas can be a very depressing time of the year. I've heard it said that suicide dramatically increases between Christmas and New Years. This seems most odd. Why would people be "down" at Christmas?

It might surprise you to realize that by the second or third Christmas the clouds gathered. Our text is filled with escapes in the middle of the night from the Bethlehem butcher, innocent babies being killed, and displacement of a young couple out on their own. I thought that Christmas was the season of perpetual joy. The bright lights and tinsel give way all too soon to the dull and sinful realities of life. The song says, "The little Lord Jesus, no crying He makes." Well, maybe, but several others did.

Matthew frames up his story about the aftermath of the magi's visit clustered around three Old Testament texts. In the story of Jesus Matthew's readers would have heard their own story. And, if they listened close, they would have heard that out of the darkest clouds God can bring newness:

I. The Child Brings New Sonship (13-15).

A. The Old Testament text is Hosiah 11:1 with overtones of Exodus 4:22. Israel was God's son. God Himself taught Israel to walk. Egypt represented a place of bondage and slavery.

B. The New Testament connection is that Jesus is the New Israel. He gives new meaning to what it means to be a son of God. Jesus is called child (He is that, not an infant, by the time the magi visit) three times in the text. As a child He is so vulnerable, but as such He teaches us to trust the Father to work everything out. Egypt for Jesus represented a place of refuge.

C. Someone said that in Jesus Christ, God was saying to the world, "Okay world, I'm going to run it by you one more time."

II. The Child Brings New Covenant (16-18).

A. The Old Testament text is Jeremiah 31:15. The people of God had been idolatrous, and God would punish them in Babylon.

The mothers of Israel wept as their children passed by the place of Rachel's tomb on route to captivity.

B.   The New Testament connection is that in Jesus God makes a new way by which people can be right with Him. History is repeating itself, and it's not pretty. There is pain in the establishment of the new way, but in the end it will blaze a trail to heaven. This is the great chapter about the new covenant, quoted extensively in Hebrews 8.

C.   Innocent children would die, perhaps as a symbol of the ugliness of man, but out of that would come the rescue of the one who would establish a new way to get home.

III. The Child Brings New Ministry (19-23).

A.   The Old Testament text is quite possibly Isaiah 11:1. Notice that Matthew doesn't quote any place in particular. He just says, "through the prophets."

B.   The New Testament connection is that with Jesus "all things become new" (2 Corinthians 5 :17). He can bring significance out of places like Nazareth. Galilee would get a chance to look at the light first. From Galilee Jesus would make His great commission at the end of the book.

C.   Someone said, "Jesus didn't come to make us better; He came to make us new." Even in His return to Galilee with His parents He inspires a new fresh start to life.

Conclusion

Christ brings newness! But with the newness sometimes comes surprises, disruptions, and pain. That's how it was with the first Christmas, and that's how it still is.

Illustrations

People usually miss the important things. In 1809 the world watched as Napoleon advanced his forces. However, in that year several babies were born that would change the course of history: William Gladstone, Alford Tennison, Oliver W. Holmes, Edgar A. Poe, Charles Darwin, and Abraham Lincoln. Don't forget to watch for the very important things, like babies.

Wholeheartedness in a Halfhearted World
Mark 1:9-39

Introduction

Many people in the Bible show the quality of wholeheartedness. Caleb wins the prize for being mentioned most about wholeheartedness. Next is Hezekiah, then Solomon, Noah, David, Daniel, and Nehemiah.

But this is in keeping with the theme of Scripture to suggest that Jesus is the supreme example of wholeheartedness. He never did anything halfway. He is the ultimate example of undistracted devotion in ministry. If we follow His example we will:

I. Jump Into Ministry (9-20).

A.   Mark records no birth announcements, no manger scenes, and no wise men. For him the good news starts with John the Baptist preaching and Jesus' jumping into ministry.

B.   Mark believes that baptism, temptations, and calling of disciples are not signs of completion of ministry but the beginning of ministry.

II. Storm Satan's Gates (21-28).

A.   The disciples must have been "struttin' while sittin' down." They had been called by Jesus and perhaps feeling quite smug.

B.   Little did they know that they would soon encounter the jaws of hell. What could be more innocent than going to the synagogue?

C.   The disciples watch as Jesus hushes the demon. No doubt they began to realize that they are on route to a genuine power encounter with the enemy. At least life with Jesus is very exciting.

III. Be Where You Are (29-34).

A.   Jesus bloomed where He was planted. When Jesus performed miracles He gave the candidate His undivided attention.

B.   Whether it was time for the sick, exorcising demons, or taking care of Peter's mother-in-law Jesus really was 100% there.

IV. Discipline Yourself in Prayer (35-39).

    A.   This is the real power behind wholeheartedness. This is the only thing that can keep us from doing ministry in the power of the flesh.

    B.   We see the time, place, habit, and even interruption to Jesus' quiet time. This has been called "altruistic egotism," i.e. permission to take care of oneself so as to be able to take care of others.

Illustrations

Be a plunger when it comes to ministry. In 1990 I had the opportunity to go swimming at Echo Lake in British Columbia. Even though it was July I was in for the surprise of my life. I had dropped the young people off at the beach, went to park the van, and then went to the bath house to change. I am persuaded that Canadians have anti-freeze for blood. I asked innocently how the water was. They smiled and winked at each other and said, "Fine, come on in." Like an idiot I ran off the end of the platform and dove into the lake. I was sure that hypothermia would set in immediately. While I came up spitting, hacking, and coughing, to the laughter of the campers, I must say it was terribly invigorating. Maybe that is the only way to do ministry. Plunge in today and be made complete.

Jesus stormed Satan's gates. Very early in the Gospel of Mark Jesus is portrayed as attacking Satan. The former great missionary Isabel Dittemore said to me once, "We don't preach on the devil any more." Perhaps she is correct. In C. S. Lewis', *The Lion, The Witch, and The Wardrobe,* the first place that the great lion, Aslan, goes after his resurrection is to the citadel of the white witch. He then breathes on the statues, and they become living beings again. What is the job of the church? To turn statues into people again. Let us get on with storming Satan's gates.

Wanted: True Worshipers

John 4:16-26

Introduction

Mission statements are everywhere. Schools have them, hospitals have them, restaurants have them, and even the license bureau has one.

It might not be wide of the mark to suggest that the chief mission of the Christian is to worship God. We see this stressed throughout the Bible:

1. In the garden we saw the test of worship.
2. Moses received 10 famous words from God which functioned as commandments of worship.
3. The Israelites were to set up the tabernacle in the middle of their encampment, no doubt showing the centrality of worship.
4. The temple was filled with smells and smoke indicating the sacrifices of worship.
5. The psalms and other works functioned as books of worship.
6. The post-exilic prophets had to try to re-institute proper worship.
7. When Christ came He showed us how important worship was by attending it regularly.
8. The early church found reason to change the day of worship.
9. The epistles functioned partly as a liturgy of worship.
10. And, Revelation ends with the rejoinder, "Worship God!"

In the encounter that Jesus had with the woman at the well we see more "worship talk" per square inch than anywhere else in the Bible.

I. Notice Who Is Talking About Worship.

A. It is not a theologian, not a Bible College professor, not a preacher, not an elder, not a Bible school teacher.

B. It is a morally wounded woman. That doesn't sound right. But maybe that is the point. The only people who will worship will be the people who sense their need to worship. At least this woman does that.

C. This morally wounded woman is undone as she talks about worship. She is the one who brings up the topic. But she is stopped in her tracks when Jesus says, "Go call your husband." Worship will never be popular, because we have to face God, and when we do that we have to face ourselves in light of God. That will undo the best of us.

II. Notice What Worship Is Not.

A. While we may want to know what worship is Jesus only defines it by the power of negation. Maybe He is more interested in us doing worship than merely defining it. In fact, one way to kill some things is to say, "Webster says. . . "

B. Worship is not:
   1. Geography . . . it can be done anywhere.
   2. Race . . . the woman was a Samaritan.
   3. Anything and everything . . . Jesus said, "You worship what you do not know." There is such a thing as wrong worship.
   4. Terminology . . . the main word here means to "bow down," but we dare not get lost in mere lexical studies.
   5. Enthusiasm . . . "in spirit" means something different than "clap your hands."

III. Notice How Worship Is Done.

A. In spirit, i.e. in sincerity of heart and attitude. While true worshipers worship God in Spirit (Philippians 3), here it is referring to a state of the heart.

B. In truth, i.e. in genuineness. Of course we want to worship God according to the Bible, but Jesus is talking about a state of the heart.

IV. Notice What Worship Leads To.

A. It leads to a further disclosure of God. The point of John 4 is not to give us a manual of personal evangelism. As the woman talks about worship with Jesus, He is revealed. This fits the Gospel's purpose (20:30-31). First she sees Him to be just a man, then a prophet, then the Messiah, and finally the Savior of the world.

B. It leads to world evangelism. Worship should always drive us into the fields of harvest. If we know Him, then we must seek to make Him known.

Conclusion

Someone once said, "A Christian should be hallelujah from head to toe." As our perception of Christ grows the only appropriate response is worship.

Building Our Lives on His Mission
Luke 4:14-30

Introduction

Jesus Christ was not fuzzy on His mission. He was entirely focused. He knew what He had to be about.

Our lives will be the more successful as we learn from Him what directed and dictated His mission.

I. Was it His Love for Fellowship (14-16)?

A. Tests often make us stronger instead of weaker. Jesus returned from his devil encounter in the power of the Holy Spirit. He was popular, He taught, and the Gospel that celebrates messianic joy recounts that everyone praised Him.

B. Bible study and prayer in a context of fellowship make us stronger instead of weaker as well. Jesus went to synagogue "as was His custom." If I had been the regular rabbi I would have wanted Him to read Scripture and exhort as well. What could you say that He didn't already know?

II. Was it His Love for the Written Word (16-22)?

A. Jesus was at home with the Bible. Without the aid of chapter divisions Jesus turned immediately to Isaiah 61 and read. Jesus found the personal application of the text to His life. Every part of the text spoke to Him and about Him.

B. Out of the Bible came direction for His mission. He found His anointing, His message, His freedom, His power, His sensitivity, and His announcement. He claimed prophetic fulfillment— something only He could do.

C. They liked it all, at least for the moment.

III. Was it His Love for all Peoples (23-30)?

A. Jesus read His audience like a book. He knew that they wanted a miracle show, and He refused to cater to such. After helping them understand His prophetic role He chose two Old Testament illustrations that drove home the point that God's care for all goes way beyond the limits of Israel. The Messiah is a missionary messiah. His care extends to the ends of the earth.

B.   Elijah cared for a woman outside of Israel, and Elisha even extended kindness to an enemy soldier of Israel. All of this was evidence of the grace of God.

Conclusion

They got the point all too well. They wanted to throw Him off the hill, but He walked out through their midst. Nothing nor no one could thwart the mission of the Messiah.

Illustrations

Say More. One mark of thorough conversion is that the Christian can rarely get enough Bible study and prayer in the context of Christian fellowship. Jesus went to the synagogue as was His custom. Good preaching should cause the people to want to go home and read the sermon text again. I wonder if any wanted to do that with Isaiah 61. It happened that way to some early missionaries. When Barnabas and Paul finished speaking in the Antioch of Pisidia synagogue the people wanted them to "say more" about these things (Acts 13:42).

The God of the outsiders. Liberation theology would have never made it to first base had there not been a grain of truth in it. The fact is, God has a heart for the oppressed and wants to set them free. We must guard carefully against a small spirit. The Jewish belief went something like this, "God had created the Gentiles to be fuel for the fires of hell." The only Gentile to write a life of Christ found great joy in his two volume set in the theme of God's all-encompassing love. The Christ of Luke 4 shows us a wide-embrace.

Live Like a King

Matthew 5:3-48

Introduction

This most famous sermon is preached more than practiced. The need is for interpretation. But the greater need is for implementation. In this sermon Jesus teaches us how to live like a king. In Matthew, Jesus is portrayed as the Son of David. Here is part of how royalty lives. To live a "cut above the world" we must live out the greater, fulfilled, real righteousness called for in this text.

I. Real Righteousness Is Described (3-12).

A. These revolutionary aphorisms congratulate the opposite of what the world applauds.

B. These revolutionary aphorisms promise God's assistance—if not now, then someday.

C. These revolutionary aphorisms have a sense of progression but not one that is hard and fast.

II. Real Righteousness Gets Exercised (13-16).

A. The irony is that the beatitude people have clout and sway.

B. The call is for the beatitude people to genuinely influence their world. There is a difference between separation from unholiness and separation from unholy people (cf. 1 Corinthians 5:10).

C. The scope for the beatitude people is universal—salt of the earth and light of the world.

III. Real Righteousness Is Examined (17-20).

A. It is directly related to Christ (17).

B. It takes God's commands very seriously (18-19).

C. It goes beyond surface requirements (20).

IV. Real Righteousness Gets Illustrated (21-47).

The six great antithesis are practical, proverbial, and check out a person quite completely.

A.   Anger is on par with murder (21 -26).

B.   Lust is on par with adultery (27-30).

C.   Divorce at all is on par with granting a divorce certificate (31-32).

D.   Simple honest words are on par with taking oaths (33-37).

E.   Kindness to enemies is on par with the law of fair play (38-42).

F.   Loving enemies is on par with loving neighbors (43-47).

Conclusion

The ultimate challenge comes in v. 48. Essentially the call to serious discipleship is the call to be like God!

The only way to really live like the King is to heed the teachings of the King.

Illustrations

Real righteousness is just that—real. In the old television show, "Leave it to Beaver," there was a classic hypocrite. His name was Eddie Haskell. He was the guy everyone loved to hate. Invariably he was the one responsible for getting Wally and Beaver in a heap of trouble. Beaver's naive loyalty was abused by Eddie. Mr. Cleaver would enter the room, and Eddie would respond in some kind of sick line like, "Hello, how are you today Mr. Cleaver, Sir?" Mr. Cleaver was wise to Eddie, but he was gracious and would respond kindly. After Mr. Cleaver would leave the room Eddie might say something to Beaver like, "Hey, what is your old man all bent out of shape for, Beaver?" One thing that the Sermon on the Mount will do if we have ears to hear is to body-slam our hypocrisy to the mat of God's grace.

Can being salt and light ever get us in trouble? "Both metaphors of salt and light raise important questions about Christian involvement in society regarding all forms of separatism or withdrawal. We are not called to control secular power structures; neither are we promised that we can Christianize the legislation and values of the world. But we must remain active preservative agents, indeed irritants, in calling the world to heed God's standards. We dare not form isolated Christian enclaves to which the world pays no attention" (Craig Blomberg, p. 103).

Straight and Broken Sticks

Matthew 11:7; 12:20

Introduction

There are two types of sticks in the world—straight ones and curved or broken ones. Likewise, there are two types of people in the world—straight ones and broken ones.

In Matthew chapters 11 and 12 there are two engaging uses of the Greek word *kalamos* (reed). John the Baptist was not a reed swayed by the wind (11:7) and Jesus came not to break a bruised reed (12:20).

I. Straight Sticks (11:7).

A.   Jesus preached a sermon about John.

    1.   John had born witness to Jesus. Now Jesus bears witness to John.

    2.   This does not mean that John was rude, belligerent, obnoxious, or just a fusser.

    3.   It does mean that when push came to shove John stood up straight and tall and told Herod that he had taken the wrong wife. He took a moral stand.

B.   What would Jesus preach about you?

    1.   Is your moral stand clear to all who hear you?

    2.   Do you wait to see which way the political wind is blowing before taking a stand?

    3.   Are you willing to go to prison like John for your convictions?

II. Broken Sticks (12:20).

A.   This is the longest quote from the Old Testament in Matthew's Gospel.

    1.   It concerns the basic character of the Messiah.

    2.   It is from Isaiah 42:1-4.

    3.   It is what God the Father says about God the Son.

B.   This is one of the most needed things in our world—compassion.

    1.   This does not mean that Jesus is soft on sin or wimpish on evil.

    2.   It does mean that Jesus learned how to take people from

where they were to where they needed to be by the power of love.

3. Jesus displayed a strong tenderness with broken folks.

Conclusion: The Real Challenge

The difficulty comes in knowing when to be tough and when to be tender, when to be a Boenerges and when to be a Barnabas, when to be a John the Baptist and when to be a physician binding wounds. To do this takes great wisdom, sensitivity, and earnest prayer.

Is possible to be both tough and tender at the same time? We really do have a word for when confrontation and compassion meet, for where justice and mercy embrace. We call it Calvary. It is not only the center our salvation; it is also the basis of how we do ministry in Jesus' name.

Illustrations

Being tough and tender at the same time. One night we were having trouble getting my ten year old to go to bed and stay. She had come to the living room several times after she had been specifically told to stay in her bed. She was quickly becoming successful at making her parents "half a step ahead of a fit." Finally, my wife went to bed. I continued to grade papers. When I finished I shut the lights down and headed to the bedroom. All of a sudden here came Annie. She said, "Daddy, you're not going to bed are you? If you go to bed I'll be the only one awake, and I'll be scared." I had just about had it. I blew up. "Young lady," I said, "You are going to bed, and you are going right now." I had been a reed not shaken by the wind. But I didn't feel very good about it. I looked down on this frightened ten year old. Her bottom lip quivered, and she began to cry. I thought for a moment and said, "You are going to bed, and you are going right now. But, Mommy already went to bed. If I go to bed now, I'll be lonely because Mommy is already asleep. Would you go to bed with me?" She smiled, and I winked at her. We walked to the bedroom, I tucked her in between my wife and me, and in about two minutes I heard a precious little snore. I thought to myself the law was satisfied—she went to bed, and she went when I told her. But she also fell asleep in her Dad's arms. I looked heavenward and thanked the Father that He found a way to be tough and tender all at the same time.

The Order of the Towel
Mark 10:45

Introduction

One old cliche says, "Familiarity breeds contempt." It doesn't have to be true, but all too often it is. We have read this text before. Can we give it a second look?

Perhaps it doesn't need interpretation as much as implementation. The accent is on following this example of our Lord:

1. It's one thing to see a leper, it's another thing to touch the leper.
2. It's one thing to hurt for the demonized, it's another thing to exorcise the demon.
3. It's one thing to sense a need to pray, it's another to spend all night in prayer.
4. It's one thing to see hungry people, it's another to feed them.
5. It's one thing to see dirty feet, it's another thing to wash them.

Servanthood: We can talk about it, idolize it, praise it, memorize it, cheer it, rally around it. But can we live it? What kind of teaching is this from our Lord?

I. It Is a Purpose Statement of His Incarnation.

A. It contrasts with negative ones:
   1. I came not to abolish the Law and the Prophets, but to fulfill them (Matthew 5: 17).
   2. I came not to bring peace (Matthew 10:34).
   3. I came not to call the righteous (Matthew 9:13).

B. It aligns itself with positive ones:
   1. I came to seek and save the lost (Luke 19:10).
   2. I came for judgment (John 9:39).
   3. I came to give life (John 10:10).

II. It Is a Positive Statement of His Ministry.

A. Did Jesus smile or frown when He said it? Does He begrudge serving or do His eyes sparkle at the prospect? This removes ministry from legalism. Jesus changes our "want to's."

B. Plato said, "How can a man be happy when he has to serve someone?" We would respond, "By having the mind of Christ."

C. Jesus didn't say this with a miserly heart.

III. It Is a Perfect Statement of His Character

    A.   The statement was made at the end of His ministry, and they (the disciples) knew that it was an accurate personal testimony.

    B.   The statement truly represented Him. There was no false egotism here. There was no, "I'm humble and proud of it."

    C.   The statement reflects what a crucified mind can do to create an environment of transformational leadership

Conclusion

There were no chief seats for James and John, but there were plenty of cups. We should be as wise as James and John and commit ourselves to being able—even before we know what true service is all about. We learn more as we serve.

Illustrations

A Towel as a Gift. When I graduated from Lincoln Christian Seminary I was part of a new tradition. Every graduate received, in addition to his or her degree and the usual hood, a towel. This was to remind the graduate that no matter what degree was behind that graduate's name it was all in vain unless the graduate joined "the order of the towel." I have appreciated this servanthood reminder through the years. I am proud of that towel. Is that right? It has the nice Lincoln Christian Seminary logo on it. I don't want to get it dirty. I might rub the logo off. Perhaps I should frame it. On the other hand, maybe Jesus wants me to wear it out.

The Joy of Service. Several years ago I received a very nice gift from my oldest son for Christmas. He had little money so the gift was one of the homemade variety. It was a set of coupons tied together with gold ribbon. Each coupon was good for some act of service. One was for washing the car (he wasn't even big enough to do that job when he promised to do it), one was for taking out the trash without being asked, and others were for other acts of kindness. I never used one of them. I thought to myself that I didn't want to take advantage of him when he was so young. However, I now see that was a mistake. I was a joy robber. He wanted to offer himself. Jesus didn't get angry at James and John for asking for chief seats. He simply redirected their spiritual ambition. Let's be willing to serve. Let's also be willing to let others serve.

The Christ, the Cross, and the New Creature

Matthew 16:13-28

Introduction

The Bible often comes at us in triads:

1. God the Father; God the Son; God the Holy Spirit.
2. Faith, hope, and love.

If you were to try and list the three most important themes of the New Testament Church which three would you mention? Eldership? Missionary commitment? Facilities? As important as these might be they might not be the most vital.

Several years ago Earnest Beam was asked to address the most important themes of the New Testament. He chose three that I would like to superimpose on this text:

I. The Christ (13-20).

A. The setting—a rocky and pagan area. A foundational truth would be spoken in an exclusive way.

B. The popular answers—John, Elijah, Jeremiah, or one of the prophets. It is never enough to just say what others say. Crowds have significant ways of being wrong at worst and being incomplete at best.

C. The issue—Christ is His office, not His last name. With six months from the cross the Lord needs to be sure that the disciples understand who He is.

II. The Cross (21-23).

A. Jesus announces the divine necessity of His suffering. "From that time on" marks a turn in the Gospel of Matthew (cf. Matthew 4:17). Now the references to the cross will not be veiled.

B. Peter objects to the "way of suffering." His temptation to Christ parallels that of the devil in chapter 4.

C. Jesus announces that suffering and the mind of God are in concert.

III. The New Creature (24-28).

A. The road to becoming a new creature is the road of self-denial.

Jesus calls for nothing short of daily denial, cross-bearing, and radical following.

B. The reasons for becoming a new creature are numerous:
   1. It is the only way to save your life (v. 25).
   2. It is the only sane perspective on what is important in life (v. 26).
   3. It is the only way to be ready for the judgment (v. 27).

C. The reality of becoming a new creature is possible by the power of God. Regardless of what v. 28 refers to, God is able to keep us alive by the power of His indestructible life.

Conclusion

Paul said, "Therefore, if anyone is in Christ, he is a new creation; the old has gone, the new has come!" (2 Corinthians 5:17).

As Jesus invites people to follow Him, He wants folks to be persuaded of who He is, understand what He did for them on the cross, and share in the excitement of this adventure of priorities called discipleship.

Illustrations

The identity of Jesus. My father often remarked that what Jesus said and did really didn't amount to much. But who He was made what He said and what He did the most important words and deeds ever recorded in the history of the universe. All things really come down to this: Who is Jesus? When people respond to Jesus Christ we don't ask them if they like our church. We ask them what they have to say about Jesus of Nazareth. How they answer that question, and how they live by their answer will be the way God will regard them in the final day.

The need for daily denial. Only Jesus can deliver us from the deadly cancer of self. Several years ago I became concerned for a wayward church member. I threw caution to the wind and decided I would confront this brother. His conversion only two years before had been most impressive. All in the community noticed the change. In the course of our conversation he said, "I don't know. I can't explain it. I guess the old man died." I quickly corrected him, "No, that is not the problem. My fear is that the old man got resurrected. Let's kill him again."

The Controversial Christ

John 7:1-52

Introduction

The Biblical Jesus is a man surrounded by controversy. He came not
to bring peace but a sword (Matthew 10:34). He is the only true cohe-
sive power in the universe and the only one who can unite all things
in Himself (Ephesians 1:10), but His truth cuts and leaves people on
one side of the fence or the other.

As early as the second Passover Jesus had aroused such enmity that
the Jews wanted to kill Him (chapter 5). Now, at the Feast of the
Tabernacles, six months prior to His final Passover, things were really
heating up. A key verse is v. 43, "Thus the people were divided
because of Jesus." Some people thought He was:
1. A good man (v. 12).
2. A deceiver (v. 12).
2. Demon-possessed (v. 20).
4. Christ (v. 26, 31, 41).
5. The prophet (v. 40).

In a sentence, the concern of this message is, "The controversy
about Christ is due to the confusion about His identity." And, that
confusion disappears only when I elect to do God's will (see v. 17).

I. Christ Encountered Controversy From His Family (1-9).

A. The unbelieving brothers urged Him to show Himself to the
world. Their fake concern could be due to jealousy, lack of dis-
cernment about His mission, or desire to cash in on His claimed
Messiahship.

B. Jesus counters by teaching lessons about timing and testimony.
The Christ is on a strict time table dictated only by the Father.
He admits that people hate Him because He reminds the world
of its evil.

II. Christ Encountered Controversy From the Crowd (10-31).

A. The crowd just couldn't get a good fix on Jesus. They entertained
all kinds of opinions about Him. Some thought He was a good
man while others thought that He was someone on the order of a
carnival leader. They questioned His credentials and His origins.

B.   Jesus counters by teaching lessons on the source of His teaching and the proof of His teaching. He reminds them to make sound judgments; not ones based on appearance only. He also reminds them of His inside track with His Father.

III. Christ Encountered Controversy From The Religious Leaders (32-52).

A.   The religious leaders (Pharisees and chief priests) had enough. They dispatched some temple police to bring Jesus in. But the guards were stopped in their tracks by Jesus' powerful words. Nicodemus attempted a slight defense but was quickly put in his place.

B.   Jesus counters by teaching lessons about His future and His offer to mankind. His future is rock solid—back home with His Father. His offer is that by belief people become recipients of the Holy Spirit, which will be poured out after Jesus is glorified.

Conclusion

The world is not totally delivered yet from the enemy's grasp. Therefore the controversy continues. Some say Jesus is the only one like God, some say that He is created by God, some say that He is not in any way like God, and others say that He is God but so is Confucious, Buddha, etc.

John the Apostle was persuaded that Jesus was the Christ, the Son of God (20:30-31).

Illustration

Christ is a person of controversy. A few years ago I was sick on a Sunday morning. That hadn't happened for about 20 years. I tried to hold my head up long enough to watch a little religious television that morning. A local congregation had a program and their special speaker that day was Oliver North. What I caught of the program was interesting to say the least. After the service concluded the local news media interviewed the local preacher. They asked him, "How could you have such a controversial figure speak in your church?" "Listen," the preacher said, "If controversy were the basis for choosing speakers for our church then Jesus Christ couldn't speak here."

The Other Love Chapter of the Bible
John 13:1-38

Introduction

Many chapters in the Bible could qualify as great chapters on the subject of love. For instance: Hosiah 11, John 3, 1 John 4. The chapter most associated with this emphasis is 1 Corinthians 13. Rightly so. There we see the importance of love (1-3), the description of love (47), and the eternality of love (8-13).

But John 13 could equally qualify as a great love chapter of the Bible. Verse 1 of this chapter says, "He showed them the full extent of his love." And, love will dominate this chapter, the entire farewell discourse, and really to the end of the Gospel, being mentioned 24 times. This emphasis on love could be carved into four sections:

I. The Example of Love (1-20).

A.   Picture this example: The God of the universe washing dirty Palestinian feet. It's a bit much to take.

B.   Think of two pairs of feet that were washed in this example.
1.   Proud Peter—have you ever tried to do something for someone too proud to receive it?
2.   Evil Judas—has anyone ever stabbed you in the back after you were kind to them? "He who shares my bread has lifted up his heel against me" (v. 18).

II. The Vulnerability of Love (21-30).

A.   This vulnerability means being open to attack, capable of being wounded. Jesus risks His neck. But that is how love is. Loving is risky business.

B.   This vulnerability is seen in the seating arrangement of the table. The arrangement is most likely in the shape of a horseshoe. Peter's feet may have been washed toward the end while Judas' may have been washed first. If this is so then Jesus had Judas sit on his left on this important night. This would demand that Jesus' head be placed in Judas' chest area. That is real love.

III. The Commandment of Love (31-35).

A.   The commandment is given when the tension eases. Judas is gone, now Jesus can relax.

B.   The commandment stems from the glory of God. Perhaps this is
      true of all of God's commandments. Since God's glory is His
      shining brilliance and His weighty presence, all his commands,
      which are for our good, come out of His person.

C.   The commandment knocks the walls out of any definition that
      would limit the scope and intensity of love. We are to love as He
      loved, and love is to be the distinguishing mark of the Christian.

IV. The Failure to Love (36-38).

A.   The failure is sad, but it will be dealt with in the next chapter
      (14:1).

B.   The failure is sad, but Peter will be reinstated for every denial (cf.
      John 21:15-23).

Conclusion

It is especially difficult to love like Jesus until we receive the love of
Jesus. Maybe that's why John 3:16 precedes John 13:34-35.

Seth Wilson said, "Christianity is not so much saying, 'I'm right,
and you're wrong,' as much as it is saying, 'I love Jesus.'" Loving God
first and most is the key to this other love chapter of the Bible.

Illustrations

How much do we look forward to washing feet? The disciples had proud
hearts and dirty feet. Contrast this with Jesus really wanting to do that
job (vs. 4-5). He thrilled at the prospect of this humiliation because
He loved His disciples. William Barclay said, "The world is full of people who are standing on their dignity when they should be kneeling at
the feet of their brethren" (p. 162).

Real love is not burdensome. Genesis 29:20 says that Jacob served Laban
another seven years for Rachel, "but they seemed like only a few days
to him because of his love for her."

The Pilgrimage of a Challenge
Luke 5:1-11

Introduction

"O to be like thee; O to be like thee, blessed redeemer, pure as thou art. Come in thy sweetness, come in thy fullness; stamp thy own image deep on my heart."

Few lines would express more clearly what real discipleship is. In a word, it is becoming like one's teacher (Luke 6:40).

Someone described discipleship as the road from the mind of the flesh to the mind of Christ. Peter shows us this pilgrimage in this seaside encounter with the living Christ:

I. First, There Is a Hesitant Obedience (v. 5).

A. Our pursuits are often fruitless without His blessing. Peter had worked hard throughout the night without success. The business of washing nets was no little thing.

B. Our hesitancy must give way to His agenda. Jesus interrupted Peter's routine.

C. Our questions are resolved when we know who He is, "Master," and we have the courage to say, "but at your word I will let down the nets."

II. Second, There Is an Honest Acknowledgment (v. 8).

A. When we see Him in His power we see ourselves in filthy rags.

B. When we obey Him in His Lordship we see ourselves as needy people.

Consider how other translations handle this verse:
1. "I'm too much of a sinner for you to have around" (TLB).
2. "Don't waste your time on a bum like me, sir!" (Cotton Patch Version).

III. Third, There Is a Wonderful Promise (v. 10).

A. We are given release from our fear. "Do not be afraid" is the phrase often on the lips of angels and deity.

B. We are given a new task. Catching men for God is nothing less than reclaiming Jesus' universe for Himself

C. We are turned into what Jesus is. His mission was to seek and to save the lost (Luke 19:10). In Him we become what we have been declared.

IV. Fourth, There Is a Willing Surrender (v. 11).

A. This surrender meant the giving up of the business. It's one thing when Jesus wants the boat to teach from (vv. 1-3). It's another thing when he wants the business as well.

B. This surrender meant total abandonment. This is a very risky place to be because you feel as if you have both feet planted firmly in mid-air, but it is what the Bible calls "walking by faith."

C. This surrender meant radical discipleship. "To follow" meant not only to literally come after but also to obey every future instruction.

Illustrations

Joy at the prospect of giving up all to follow Jesus. David Livingstone, the great missionary from Scotland said, "He is the greatest master I have ever known. If there is anyone greater, I do not know him. Jesus Christ is the only master supremely worth serving. He is the only ideal that never loses its inspiration. He is the only friend whose friendship meets every demand. He is the only Savior who can save to the utter-most. We go forth in His name, in His power, and in His Spirit to serve Him."

When we get a clear view of Jesus we see ourselves for who we are. Several years ago my father made a follow up call on a family whose children had come to VBS. It was a simple "thank you" call. Later the father of that home revealed to my dad that when my dad had left, the man went to the refrigerator, pulled out his bottle, and dumped the contents down the sink. My father was surprised and mentioned that no discussion was made concerning such things. The man responded, "I know that. But I could see that what you were inviting me to was so opposed to the way I was living I had no other choice." So it is with every honest person. That man later went on to become an elder in the church.

The Call to Adventure

Matthew 4:18-22

Introduction

Someone said, "Christians are like stoplights on a car. They never do anything until you stomp on them real hard, and then they turn red all over." I don't believe it. It seems to me that many want to be serious disciples, but they are lost as to what is involved.

Stuart Briscoe says that disciples in the ancient world were made in several ways. Teachers made disciples by way of protest, procedure, and principles. But Jesus made disciples "personally." In fact, he says, "The test of one's discipleship is the depth of one's relationship."

To probe the depths of one's relationship we can look to the calling of the four fishermen. In that story we see three descriptions of discipleship. Genuine following of Christ means:

I. Attachment to His Person.

A. The disciples could literally do this. To "come after" Christ was real. They could literally follow Him where He went. Two sets of brothers follow now. Matthew will come by chapter 9, and all the disciples will be in place by chapter 10.

B. We can spiritually do this. While the call of Jesus is not privatistic, it is personal. We really can follow Him in obedience.

C. In Christianity it is not enough to agree with the teachings; one must fall in love with the teacher himself. It would be hard to imagine doing this without a genuine commitment to reading the Gospels.

II. Surrender to His Will.

A. For Peter, Andrew, James, and John this meant a vocational shift of significant proportions. Perhaps it meant that father Zebedee had to look elsewhere for heirs to his business.

B. For us it means yielding—perhaps even our career choices (cf. James 4:13-17) This doesn't mean that everyone who responds to the call of Christ for salvation and service must enter vocational labor for Christ, but it does mean that we are willing to if that is what He wants.

C. In Christianity the first pre-requisite for discipleship is to deny self. This is the only road to Christian joy. From Jesus' point of view letting God rule our lives is a wonderful thing—something on the order of a treasure hidden in a field or a pearl merchant on search for fine pearls (Matthew 13:44-46).

III. Acceptance of His Mission.

A. For the disciples this meant to start fishing for people. The imagery deals with evangelism, church growth, and the missionary enterprise of the church. Perhaps the book of Acts is the best commentary on this.

B. For us it means to emotionally own the world that God loves. This would affect our prayers, our giving, our time, and the total stewardship of our lives.

C. In Christianity there is one word for all of this: GO ! The calling of the disciples in chapter 4 prepares the twelve for their short-term missions trip in chapter 10, which in turn gets them ready for the great commission of chapter 28. God calls us to Himself so that He can send us out. The God of the Bible is a pilgrim God who is always on the move.

Conclusion

The call to adventure demands total commitment. The disciples struggled with this as we will. But we can work at becoming totally committed. Therein lies the adventure. Attachment, surrender, and acceptance—those are the keys.

Illustrations

Surrendering our will is so hard. I know of nothing as personally challenging as surrendering one's will. It goes against everything in post-modern times. We selfishly cling to that which will kill us. The number one hit in the Garden of Eden was, "I Did It My Way." But this path leads only to death, and many there are that find it. We should take great joy at prospect of the government of God. "I did it my way" must yield to "sweet will of God."

Unconditional Surrender

Luke 9:57-62

Introduction

Someone said, "The Holy Spirit won't manifest Himself until we deny ourselves." This is a real key to following Christ. We must do spiritually speaking what the Japanese did militarily speaking on September 2nd aboard the U.S.S. Missouri. We must sign on with an "unconditional surrender."

People who really love God welcome the opportunity to reassess their commitment to Him. People who haven't fallen in love with Christ usually squirm in the pew when we approach the "would-be" disciples. What did the "disciple wanna-be's" learn in this text?

I. To Follow Christ There Can Be no Earthly Securities (57-58).

A.   The man offers the presumptuous challenge. It sounds like a "no strings attached" commitment. We want to stand and applaud him.

B.   But Jesus responds in personal testimony with highly figurative language. Foxes and birds have homes, but the Son of Man holds on to nothing in this fallen world as a security blanket. In fact the only earthly home that Jesus had was a cross (cf. John 19:30).

II. To Follow Christ There Can Be no Prior Loyalties (59-61).

A.   Jesus waits for no presumptuous remark this time. He engages the man, "Follow me." The challenge is for the man to radically rearrange his life in obedience to Christ.

B.   This second candidate asks to bury his father first. The third candidate says he will follow, "but . . ." Both men had the prior loyalty of family. Jesus' strange remark about dead people burying dead people shows that He doesn't like to receive an indefinite postponement of commitment.

III. To Follow Christ There Can Be no Half-Hearted Duties (62).

A.   The would-be disciples might have been miserable in Christ's service because they would want to keep one foot in the world and one foot in the Kingdom of God.

B.	To long for other things while in the Kingdom of God is a contra-diction in terms and could even turn one into a pillar of salt. The Kingdom of God is the major teaching of this unique part of Luke's Gospel (chapters 9-19). To have it with half of a heart is like asking for a peanut-butter and jelly sandwich at a Thanksgiving dinner.

Conclusion

I have never found it easy to be a Christian, but I have consistently found it to be best. Jesus wants no summer-time soldiers or fair-weather disciples. Let's do whatever it takes!

Illustrations:

Jesus is not anti-family, He is just pro-God. Twelve years ago Ozark Christian College had a special honor on behalf of her beloved Dean, Seth Wilson. Thousands came to share in the special joy. Nine of the ten Wilson children were there to help all of the rest of us celebrate. At one point, Carl Wilson said to the crowd about his father, "I think Dad didn't love us less; I think he just loved God more." The irony of it all is that when we put Jesus first, even before family, we become the best husbands and fathers and the best wives and mothers.

Don't approach the Christian life or Christian work with half of a heart. The young man who served as the best man in our wedding grew up on a farm in southwest Missouri. One day his dad told him to go cultivate the beans. That was the last thing he wanted to do. He wanted to sit in his room and listen to his stereo. To say that cultivating beans was not on his list of priorities would be to make a profound understate-ment. He went, but he went very reluctantly. He was so disgusted with his lot that he turned the tractor radio to full blast and quickly got into the beat more than into the job. When he got to the end of the field he looked back and noticed that he had plowed up eight rows of beans. His dad was not a happy camper. Half-heartedness doesn't work well on the farm or in the Kingdom of God.

The Government of God Is Worth It

Matthew 13:45, 46

Introduction

Jesus wrapped some of his most significant teachings about the Kingdom in parable form. Parables, like jokes, have good punch-lines. The eight parables in Matthew 13 (Jesus' third great discourse in Matthew—all of which is in parable form) are no exceptions. Jesus invites us to understand the mysteries of the kingdom of heaven.

Jesus describes the kingdom in terms of its results (sower and soils), in terms of its reality (mustard seeds and leaven), in terms of revelation (weeds and wheat as well as the drag-net), and in terms of relevance (hidden treasure and pearl merchant).

The context is at least engaging. Jesus packages two parables that show the worth of God's rule in our lives between two sections that deal with the end time. Perhaps the arrangement says to us that the value we place on God's reign now may determine our own end time. In some way God's rule in us is like a pearl merchant:

I. The Merchant Sought the Pearl, and the Kingdom is Worth Searching For.

A. People may have to search to find the kingdom. This is not true for everyone. Some find the kingdom almost accidentally, like the man plowing in the former parable. But others find it after an intense search. Think of Anna (Luke 2), the eunuch (Acts 8), Cornelius (Acts 10), the people of Berea (Acts 17), Justin Martyr, Tischendorf, and others.

B. The good news of the early preachers is that this kingdom can be found once this search is started (Acts 17:27). Jesus pronounced a word of congratulations on those who hungered for it (Matthew 5:6) and on those who sought it first (Matthew 6:33).

II. The Merchant Sacrificed for the Pearl, and the Kingdom is Worth Sacrificing For.

A. People sacrifice for all kinds of worthy endeavors. Some give themselves to the fight against pornography, others take their stand against abortion, and still others fight abuse and alcoholism. These are worthy pursuits.

B.   The good news is that the kingdom shines brighter than all of these things. Nothing else compares to the reign of God in our hearts. We should rejoice in the privilege of making such a deal as to sell everything else in order to know Him (Philippians 3).

III. The Merchant Secured the Pearl, and the Kingdom is Worth Securing.

A.   People sometimes try to enjoy the reign of God by long distance. They may search, and they may even be willing to make some level of sacrifice. But until that point they can still go back to their former desires. But once the transaction is complete they live with the reality of that decision.

B.   The good news is that the pearl merchant thought he had made a great deal. Like Archimedes in 250 B.C. yelling, "Eureka," the pearl merchant felt that he had indeed found it.

Conclusion

Let us thrill with the prospect of making such a transaction. Perhaps it will be like the little girl reciting the 23rd Psalm. She didn't quite get it right. She said, "The Lord is my shepherd, that's all I want." Then again, maybe she did get it right.

Illustrations

People who forgot the value of sacrifice. Two men in the Bible illustrate the lack of willingness to sacrifice for the right thing. In the Old Testament Esau takes the prize. Like some of the busters of the present generation the only word he knows is, "Now." A mess of beans looked better than a future with his father's blessing. In the New Testament the Rich Young Ruler wins. When he saw what the kingdom cost he went away with his face fallen. Jesus respected his autonomy and didn't chase after him, but He did go to preach to the disciples and crowd about making poor choices—like choosing money over entering the kingdom.

Do we enjoy the prospect of the exchange? Seth Wilson has remarked about this passage, "Are we eager to sell all also to have Him rule our lives? And, how great is our joy of the opportunity to make the trans-action?" (p. 227). There is something refreshing in our day of a plethora of activities to find someone with the power of purpose, like Paul, who could say, "This one thing I do . . ." (Philippians 3).

Enlarging Your Circle of Love

Luke 10:25-37

Introduction

The older I get the more I realize the truthfulness of the old adage, "All truths are equally true, but not all truths are of equal importance." Said in a little different way for those of us who study Scripture, "All Bible verses are inspired, but not all Bible verses are created equal." God has His own way of underlining the big things of the book.

One of the biggest things in the book is love. The texts that speak about love can be clustered in three areas: God's love for us, our love for God, and His love in us for others. It is this third area where the rub comes.

The lawyer in our text had made his circle of love, and he didn't like Jesus pushing the limits of that love. But if this text says anything then it says that love for others, especially those in need, cannot be limited in scope and intensity.

When we love with limits and qualifications we will:
1. Try to test Jesus instead of learn from Him (v. 25).
2. Have a legalistic view of salvation (v. 25).
3. Ask questions we already know the answer to (v. 26-27).
4. Have trouble making our walk the same as our talk (v. 28).
5. Attempt to justify ourselves (v. 29).

When we love without limits we will:

I. Love Even Those Who Have Been Careless (30).

A.   The man had traveled the "Bloody Way." Perhaps it was night, and perhaps he had been alone. If either of those things are true, then he is an idiot.

B.   Do we have to help people who have only themselves to blame for their difficulty? Haven't you ever wanted to say to someone, "Well, you made your own mess; now just sit in it."

II. Love Even When Those We Love Haven't Been Loved by Others (31-32).

A.   The man was viewed by two religious men, and they chose to pass by on the other side. Keep in mind that the priest and Levite were not evil men. They were leaders of the Jewish community that others should want to imitate.

B. Do we have to love those who have failed to receive help from Christian leadership?

III. Love Even When Those We Love are our Enemies (33).

A. The man was a Samaritan. For the only Gentile to write a life of Christ that was a significant detail. The Samaritans had refused Jesus lodging in the last chapter. Why would Jesus paint those people as the good guys?

B. Do we really have to love our enemies into being our friends? Why can't we only greet those who greet us?

IV. Love Even When Those We Love are Disgusting (34a).

A. The man didn't look very good. He had been in a struggle and was left for dead. The Samaritan acts medicinally and compassionately.

B. Do we have to love those who might turn our stomachs? Surely there must be a limit somewhere. Trained professionals might be able to do this, but "I don't have the stomach for it."

V. Love Even When Those We Love Cost Time and Money (34b-35).

A. The man interrupted the Samaritan's schedule. I doubt seriously if the Samaritan's day-timer read, "Help bloody people today." The Samaritan changed his entire agenda and sacrificed some big bucks to help.

B. Do we have to put our money where our mouth is when it comes to real loving?

Conclusion

For the Samaritan to be portrayed as the hero shows Luke's emphasis on the heart of God to include all people! And, the parable won't set you free! It puts you under obligation: "Go and do likewise."

The Strange Offense of God's Grace

Matthew 20:1-16

Introduction

Some people are offended by the miracles of the Bible. What should serve to engender and enlarge faith becomes for them a stumbling block.

I might be naive, but I have never been offended by the miracles of the Bible. It always seemed rational to me that if God existed, and if God was really God, then He could do everyone of those things that the book talked about.

But sometimes I confess that I am offended by the grace of God. And, evidently I am not the only one. This parable might be the strongest statement on the grace of God found anywhere in the New Testament in parable form. We can view it from three perspectives:

I. The Perspective of Those Paid First: Surprised by Joy.

A. Keep in mind that these were hired last. They are not naturally innocent (vs. 6), but they are "Johnny come lately." In simple, almost naive trust, they go into the vineyard to work.

B. When they are paid they are "surprised by joy." No doubt they are overwhelmed by the generosity of the landowner. There's probably nothing they wouldn't do for him. They are no doubt kicking themselves for putting off working in the vineyard so long.

II. The Perspective of Those Paid Last: Where's the Beef?

A. Keep in mind that these were hired first. Not only did they bear the burden of the heat of the day, but they also had to stand in line to get paid.

B. When they are paid they must have wanted to say, "Where's the beef?" They are overwhelmed by the generosity of the landowner as well, and they don't like it. They can't rejoice in other's successes, which may speak volumes about where they are spiritually.

III. The Perspective of the Landowner: Amazing Grace.

A. Keep in mind his many good attributes:

1. He is avid in recruiting laborers for his harvest.
2. He is earnest about getting his crop in.
3. He is just. He pays what he says he will pay.
4. He is tactful when unjustly attacked. He calls his accusers, "Friend" (the same word Jesus uses for Judas later).

B. But most of all the outstanding characteristic of this landowner is his grace. He wants to give to many the same. He delights in surprising people.

Conclusion

The immediate context helps us see that the offense of grace is removed when I capture the heart of the landowner. Peter just mentioned that the disciples had left all to follow Jesus, and he wanted to know what they would get. Jesus answers that they will occupy important places, but the kingdom of heaven is really all about grace In 20:17-19 Jesus predicts the cross, which is the great leveler of us all In 20:20-28 James and John have to learn that grace includes servanthood and humility.

We really don't get salvation the old fashioned way. We don't "earn it." We get it the same way the grateful and the grumblers got it—by grace. When we understand this we will:

1. Work hard but be delivered from workacholism.
2. Have compassion for all people.
3. Be delivered from a spirit of partiality.
4. Rest in God and have his peace.

I am real glad that the Father in heaven still throws parties for prodigals, because one day He threw a party for me.

Illustration

The sin of a small heart. At least two people in the Bible illustrate a miserly heart. In the Old Testament Jonah is commissioned to go to Nineveh and preach. After resisting God's call, he finally goes and the people repent—but Jonah is upset!

In the New Testament Jesus told a story about a man who had two sons. The younger took his inheritance, traveled to a far country, and squandered it. He found repentance in a pig pen and came home. His father greeted him and threw a party. But the elder brother could not rejoice in the grace of the Father.

Maybe the test of whether or not you have really received grace is "can you be gracious?"

Miracles: Previews of Coming Attractions
Mark 6:56

Introduction

Jesus Christ was no mere slight-of-hand magician. He was, in the truest sense, a worker of wonders. The Gospels do not have an unhealthy interest in miracles, but they give us plenty of miraculous evidence to believe in Jesus.

Two qualifications about Jesus' miraculous works should be made:
1. Miracles do not appear in every page of Christ's life. They are exceptions to the norm.
2. Miracles are not self-authenticating. They do not ensure belief (Mark 6:5-6). They should help engender faith (John 10:38; 20:30-31), but they can get in the way of faithful progress (John 6:26).

The issue before us in our text is that all that came to Jesus were healed. I would like to ask why. For what reason did our Lord work miracles, signs, wonders, and works?

I. To Show His Identity (Mark 2:10).

A.   There is a tight relationship between a miracle and the Messiah. Jesus healed the paralytic's sickness to prove that He could solve the man's bigger problem of sin.

II. To Demonstrate that the Kingdom had Come (Matthew 12:28).

A.   There is a tight relationship between the reign of God being re-established on planet earth and the Messiah. Casting out demons was a sign that the end of the age had come.

III. To Extend Kindness (Matthew 8:4).

A.   Sometimes Jesus worked miracles just because He wanted to. His heart went out to hurting folk. No doubt the leper welcomed the words, "I am willing." His heart is touched with my grief.

IV. To Stir Controversy (John 5:1-18).

A.   There is a tight relationship between miracle and mess. Miracles can make things very messy. They can get the miracle worker in a heap of trouble, especially if they are done on Saturday. It may sound odd to our ears, but Jesus sometimes worked miracles to stir up the people so that they would be forced to deal with His deity and claims.

V. To Reward Faithfulness (Mark 7:24-30).

A. There is an interesting relationship between faith and miracles. It is not an absolute relationship. Faith is not always required for a miracle for a very simple reason—God is sovereign. To the woman who was a definite outsider (a dog) the miracle proved a reward of her faith.

VI. To Fulfill Prophecy (Matthew 8:17).

A. There is a tight relationship between predictive prophecy and the Messiah. It was said that when He came the deaf would hear, the blind would see, and the lame would leap like a deer.

VII. To Pour Out the Glory of God (John 11:4).

A. There is a tight relationship between Jesus' whole life and the glory of God. When He walked among us we beheld the glory of God. When people saw Lazarus walking around all they could say was, "Glory to God."

Conclusion

But beyond any of these purposes, miracles are part of Christ's saving work! As Jesus worked miracles He began to save the world. Miracles are not just proofs of deity, and therefore should not be approached apologetically only. The miracle stories of the Bible have salvation talk in them. "Faith", "save", and "mercy" are words that appear in the miracles. They are cameos of life in the new heaven and new earth. They are snapshots of future glory. When a miracle takes place the recipients have a brief glimpse into a future world ruled totally by God where there is no sickness, death, or oppression by the evil one.

Illustration

Miracles and the movies. Going to the movies might be an appropriate metaphor to understand miracles. Before the feature presentation there are usually some previews of coming attractions. So it is with Christ's miracles during His first coming.

A Progression of Power
Mark 4:35—5:43

Introduction

Miracles are a display of the mighty power of God. If you can understand this in a context of reverence, miracles are when God "struts His stuff." It allows Him to show off. However, His character keeps Him from doing so in ways that would appear proud.

Miracles, like parables, often occur in clusters. When they do we should look for "end stress," i.e. the accent will be on the last one. Such is the case in this text of three (or four) miracles.

I. Jesus Has Power Over Creation (4:35-41).

A. A question is asked in panic—"Teacher, don't you care if we drown?" It is a most odd question in light of his journey from heaven to earth to specifically care for mankind.

B. A question is formed in rebuke—"Why are you so afraid? Do you still have no faith?" I can understand why they were afraid. It is one thing to face a storm, it is quite another to face the living God of the universe in a small boat.

C. A question is left to be pondered—"Who is this? Even the wind and waves obey him!" They entertain the prospect of His deity. The crowds will do the same in chapter seven (v. 37), and finally the disciples will openly confess it in chapter eight (v. 29).

II. Jesus Has Power Over the Spirit World (5:1-20).

A. The demons plead for Jesus to send them away, so He grants their wish. Imagine the transition here—out of the storm and into the jaws of hell. Graveyards and naked men—what a sight!

B. The people plead for Jesus to leave, so He does. He is a gentleman of the highest order. He will not stay where He is not welcome.

C. The delivered man pleads to go with Jesus, but he refuses. How strange! The demons get their wish, the people get their wish, but the reclaimed man is told to go home and witness.

III. Jesus Has Power Over Illness/Death (5:21-43).

A. Here is a story within a story. Three things tie these stories together:

1. The events really happened this way. The Gospel testimony seems consistent.

2. The age of the little girl and the number of years the woman has been ill.

3. The fact that both women are referred to as "daughter."

B. Here is a strong progression. If Jesus can calm an out-of-sorts creation, and if He can take on the demons of hell, surely He can handle our number one problem: illness and its ultimate end, death.

Conclusion

Not everything is a miracle. They are special, unique, and rare. But when they happen they display the power of God like fireworks on the fourth of July.

Illustrations

Faith has all kinds of questions. A preacher visited a young people's Bible school class one Sunday. As a way to engage the class he asked the students, "Okay, who can tell me what faith is?" Several answers were given. Finally one little girl said, "Faith is believing God without asking any questions." That is a good answer, if you are a little girl in Sunday School. But anyone who has any maturity in Jesus realizes that faith has within it many questions. And, it should. Doubts are allowed to exist in a context of reverence and faith. And, all of our questions of faith disappear when we focus clearly on the object of faith, Jesus Christ.

Rebukes in question form. Jesus rebuked the disciples in question form. It can be done, and in fact, parents do it all the time. It really can be a delightful way to teach. I might say to one of my four children, "Hey, didn't I tell you to get in that room and pick up those toys?" That might come out as a question, but it really is a rebuke or even a command. Perhaps this tells us something about the grace of God. Even when He needs to rebuke us, He finds a loving way to do it.

Acknowledging the Lordship of Christ   6.

Matthew 21:23-27

Introduction

Authority has fallen on hard times in the Western World. Ever since "The Fonz," with his leather jacket, rode his harley into Arnolds authority is not something to acknowledge but to resist.

And, it really goes back farther than that. Man has had a challenging time acknowledging God's reign since the Garden of Eden. God is vulnerable enough to allow such rebellion, but the story of the Bible is, as one man put it, "To get back what rightfully belongs to Him."

I. Certain Events Acknowledge Christ's Lordship (21:1-22).

A.   Three events emphasize this Lordship: The triumphal entry emphasizes that He is king of the city (1-11). The cleansing of the temple emphasizes that He is king of the temple (12-17). The cursing of the fig tree emphasizes that He is king of creation (18-22).

B.   These categories exist today and, for those who have eyes to see, Christ's lordship can still be seen—in the world at large, in religious life, and in all of nature.

II. Certain Teachings Acknowledge Christ's Lordship (21:28—22:14).

A.   Jesus came to a stand off with the religious leaders and said that He wouldn't tell them by what authority He operated. However, in the veiled method of parables He does tell them:
1.   The parable of the two sons emphasizes repentance (28-32).
2.   The parable of the tenants emphasizes rejection (33-46).
3.   The parable of the wedding banquet and garment emphasizes rebellion (22: 1-14).

B.   These responses exist today and, for those who have ears to hear, Christ's lordship will cause the most unlikely to repent, the religious elite to humble themselves and not think more highly of themselves than they ought, and outsiders to remind themselves that they stand in the kingdom by grace and cannot come in on their own terms.

III. Certain Questions Acknowledge Christ's Lordship (22:15-40).

A. Three questions emphasize this lordship:

   1. A political question: Shall we pay taxes or not (15-22)?
   2. A theological question: What is resurrected life like (23-33)?
   3. An ethical question: Which is the greatest commandment (34-40)?

B. These same questions exist today: How does the government of God and the government of people go together? What does the future hold? And is there some umbrella principle that holds all of life together?

Conclusion

Jesus gets the last laugh. The question raised by the chief priests and elders focuses the issue of authority (our text). The question raised by Jesus focuses the issue of identity (22:41-46). The broad sweeps of our text begin on Palm Sunday and end on Tuesday of the final week. The humble king rides into town for the show down on Sunday. By Tuesday He has focused the issue on the fact that He really is the Son of David.

Illustrations

Does it matter who Jesus is? I have heard Tom Ewald from Lincoln Christian College and Seminary describe the country of Germany in ways that make one say, "What one believes about Jesus affects everything else." At one point in German history the people of that country believed that the Bible was the Word of God and that Jesus was the Son of God. This is not to say that every person in the country was a Christian but that the mindset and world-view was fixed on those realities at their center. Out of that period of history Germany produced some of the greatest names in the histories of the arts—Bach and Beethoven to mention only two. However that same country later in time failed to believe and to live Christ's lordship, and they gave the world the second world war. It does matter what you believe and how you acknowledge Christ.

Ashamed or Approved?

Matthew 25:1-46

Introduction

One man asked a Christian, "What would you be if you weren't a Christian?" The Christian responded, "I'd be ashamed of myself." Amen!

On the other hand, what does it feel like to be approved? You feel stroked, affirmed, good, and like your self-esteem could reach to the heavens.

In the second half of the great eschatological speech of Jesus there are three objective ways to know whether one will receive approval or shame when Jesus comes again. One story deals with women, one with men, and one with animals. Here is the grid-iron test:

I. Be Ready (1-13).

A. Five were not foolish because they fell asleep. Perhaps no one expected the delay. Five were not wise because they were not generous. Perhaps they really didn't have enough oil for the others.

B. The real point is that we cannot buy someone else's preparation.

II. Be Faithful (14-30).

A. The one was not criticized because he only had one talent. Each man had received in accordance to his ability (v. 15). The other two were not commended because of partiality on the part of the master. Actually they had risked all that the master had given them. That was quite a risk.

B. The real point is that God can be trusted, but can you? This parable turns the whole Bible on its ear. Are you reliable? And, are you reliable now? There is an immediacy in the parable. No one knows when the master is coming.

III. Be Loving (31-46).

A. The sheep are not commended because they had the concept of working for their commendation. In fact, they were surprised when they were commended. The goats are not condemned because they were evil. They were just not sensitive to the hurts of the brothers, whoever that might be.

B.   The real point is that the King who does the separating at the end
     of the age wants to see real hard-core evidence that we love Him
     by loving others. This love is measurable. It is objective and tangi-
     ble. You can chart when you feed someone or when you give
     someone a drink, when you invite someone into your house or
     clothe someone, or even when you visit someone in prison.

Conclusion

You don't have to be a rocket scientist to choose approval or being
ashamed. Choose wisely and be ready for His coming. Heaven is a
prepared place for prepared people!

Illustrations

Don't have a puny spirit and misrepresent your master when he comes.
When the great missionary, J. Russell Morse, died a memorial service
was held for him in our chapel. B.A. Austin told, as part of the service,
about a time when Brother Morse went with him to a minister's meet-
ing. Here was a man who had been in a communist prison, lied to and
about, and practically starved to death. The ministers started sharing
about some of their pet peeves in the ministry. Several answers were
given like unjustified criticism, unrealistic expectations, ignorant people, etc. Mr. Morse was the last to speak—probably providentially. He
said, "Gentlemen, I have many peeves in the ministry, but I try hard
never to pet them." Such characterizes this great man of God. The
wicked, lazy, and worthless servant pet his peeves and was not ready
when the master came. Let us not have a small spirit and share in the
man's fate.

What hurts Christ. A young disciple said to his Jewish rabbi once, "My
master, I love you." The rabbi responded, "Do you know what hurts
me, my son?" The disciple looked bewildered and said that he didn't
understand. The rabbi said, "How can you love me if you don't know
what hurts me?" Christ is hurt by our many insensitivities. Remember
what Harry Farra said, "Horizontal sensitivity is the key that unlocks
the door to vertical grace" (Harry Farra, p. 170).

Putting Your Faith on the Line

Mark 14:32-42

Introduction

Many people in the Bible put their faith on the line for God. They showed us that there is a certain element of risk involved in faith: Judah (Genesis 44), Esther (Esther 4), Peter (Matthew 14).

But none is as impressive as Jesus Christ. He put his faith on the line several times, but the garden of Gethsemane was a moment worthy of mention. For Christ, putting His faith on the line meant resolving to do the will of God, even if it meant a cross. We see this in the drama in the garden. Adam and Eve had failed in a garden, but Jesus will succeed.

I. We See Faith on the Line in a Haunting Place (32).

A. This place was often inviting. The disciples gathered here often (cf. John 18:2). No doubt it served as a place of refuge during that difficult week. The disciples could unwind here while Jesus prayed. But not tonight. Those old gnarly olive trees were more spooky than inviting.

B. Our place is often not inviting either. Maybe because it is too distracting to do serious business for God. Our place might be a dining room table, a kitchen stool, a bedroom chair, or a patio deck. Maybe we need to find a garden this week.

II. We See Faith on the Line in the Midst of Disappointing Partners (33a, 37-40).

A. Jesus wants to be alone to pray, and yet He wants the close association of at least three of his disciples. This is one of the most ironic parts of the text. It is truly ambivalent. He takes the inner three not because Jesus plays favorites, but because they need to be the closest to Him. Peter had just pledged unconditional loyalty, and the sons of thunder said that they could drink the cup, which Jesus will pray to have removed.

B. Our dilemma when we put our faith on the line is that we often have to do it alone. People will let you down often when you are in a crunch. Jesus knew what we must learn—that is, only God the Father is with you all the time.

III. We See Faith on the Line Through Intense Pain (33b-35).

A. Everything hurts in this text. There is painful posture, painful time, and painful vocabulary. Jesus is "surrounded by sorrow."

B. Rarely do we advance in faith without difficulty. One of the strongest teachings in Scripture for believers is that they are incomplete without the benefit of trials (cf James 1:2f, 1 Peter 1:6).

IV. We See Faith on the Line Through Earnest Prayer (36).

A. Perhaps this is the key to the whole text. Jesus resolves to do the will of God in the context of prayer. In this prayer we see:
1. An enduring acknowledgement—Abba, Father.
2. A frustrating admission—all things are possible to you.
3. A dynamic request—let this cup pass from me.
4. An absolute resolution—not what I will, but what you will.

B. Our resolutions for God are cemented when they are done in prayer. If Jesus learned obedience through what He suffered, and He learned it by offering up prayers and tears to God (Hebrews 5:7), what makes us think that it will be any different for us?

Conclusion

God never spoke that Thursday evening. But Jesus interpreted the silence correctly—He must go to the cross. But He was now ready. He faced His betrayer and His enemies courageously. He was truly a different man coming out of the garden than He was when he went in.

Illustrations

Sometimes we gain victory through pain. I was watching Monday night football several years ago when Walter Payton was still running the ball for the Chicago Bears. On one particular play he made a long gain and was pushed out of bounds. They stopped the game and gave him the ball. The announcer said, "Can you believe that? With that rush Walter Payton has gained nine miles of rushing yardage." The other sports commentator broke in, "Yeah, and that's something when you consider that he got knocked down every 4.5 yards." We will get knocked down, but we can gain the victory.

Faylure
Matthew 26:69—27:25

Yes, the title is misspelled! But it is done so on purpose! That's the way it is when we fail.

Sometimes when we fail it is no big deal. In fact, a measure of our mental health might be the ability to laugh at ourselves. However, some failures are not funny at all. They bite like a viper.

In our text, Matthew arranges, in topical fashion, three failures in a row. None of the other Gospels have this exact arrangement. Perhaps in the failures of others Matthew found his own story as a former tax collector. And when man was failing at his worst God was succeeding at His best. Let us work backwards through the text:

I. Pilate Failed Because he was Overwhelmed by Peer Pressure (27:11-25).

A. He could have gone down in history as the most judicious procurator. He could have stopped this crazy kangaroo court. But he caved in. He attempted several different things:
1. He questioned the accused personally.
2. He tried to substitute Barabbas, thinking that the crowd would never want him.
3. He listened ambivalently to his wife's note.
4. He appealed to the crowd to change their verdict. But in the end, he bowed to peer pressure.

B. We sometimes forget who the real majority is. Don't be like the leaders of the Jews. They wanted to believe in Jesus but were afraid of being put out of the synagogue, "for they loved praise from men more than praise from God" (John 12:42-43). God is the real majority.

II. Judas Failed Because he was Overwhelmed by Extreme Sorrow (27:1-10).

A. He could have turned his life around, but he made poor choices. At first, things look so good:
1. He felt remorse. It's not the same as repentance, but it is a start.
2. He returned the money—some evidence of repentance. He confessed—I have sinned. But then hanged himself.

B.   We sometimes forget that God is bigger than our troubles. In the end, only He can dig us out of our pits. In fact, sometimes it is in the midst of our weaknesses that we find His strength (2 Corinthians 12:1).

III. Peter Failed Because he was Overwhelmed With Excessive Pride (26:69-75).

A.   He had the chance to really "stand up for Jesus." Instead, because he was set on his own agenda, he was intimidated by a little slave girl. It is amazing what undoes us when we are outside the will of God. His talk gave him away. In a spiritual sense that is true of all of us.

B.   But in contrast to Pilate and Judas, Peter came back. His road back after failure looks like this:
1.   He remembered the word of the Lord.
2.   He manifested a spirit of brokenness.
3.   He, in contrast to Judas, stayed in the group. When we fail the hardest people to face are church people. But they are the only ones who can truly restore us.

Conclusion

The Bible is full of people who fail, because that is the only type of people that there are. Our God specializes in hitting straight licks with crooked sticks. He is the God of grace and the God of the second chance. May this inspire us to pray for the power to overcome when temptation comes near as opposed to always being content to pray for forgiveness after knowing that we'd fail.

Illustrations

"I've done things I never thought I could do". I counseled a young girl once who detailed an affair with a neighbor man by which she had become pregnant. She walked into my office having just come from an abortion clinic and wanted me to go with her to detail everything to her husband. I will never forget her opening line. In terrible hurt and through many tears she said, "I've done things I never thought I had the capacity to do." I thought to myself that if you changed the details all of us could say that. Aren't we all amazed at the level of evil in us?

Catch the Spirit of Calvary

Mark 15:21-39

Introduction

The Gospel writers present the story of Calvary's love in such a way that the reader feels uniquely present and somehow strangely responsible. For what happened that day was bigger than history.

The Gospel writers put the accent not on the gore of the cross but on the eternal realities that took up time and space that day. If we discern those spiritual realities we will really catch the spirit that motivates Calvary.

I. He Refused to be Helped so we Could be Helped by God (21-27).

A. There were some things that God had to do by Himself. He could have called 10,000 angels, but He didn't. This emphasizes the great self-limitation of God. The subject of the sentences in this paragraph is "they."

B. There are many ironies in this paragraph:
1. He was helped by an ethnic whose agenda got interrupted (v. 21).
2. He was crucified on a skull of a hill where He would bruise the enemy's head (v. 22).
3. He was offered a narcotic in an hour of trial, but unlike so many He refused to take it (v. 23).
4. He was saving the world while it played a game of chance (v. 24).
5. He was crucified at an hour of prayer (v. 25).
6. He was charged with being who He was as His crime (v. 26).
7. He was crucified between two thieves, the kind of people He had spent lots of time with in His ministry (v. 27).

II. He Refused to Save Himself so we Could be Saved (25-32).

A. This wonderful truth is announced by the crowd. In words very close to Psalm 22 people shook their heads, taunted Him about the temple, cried out for Him to save Himself. Sometimes the gospel comes out of the strangest places.

B. This wonderful truth is also announced by the religious leaders such as the chief priests and teachers of the law. Their mockery is indicative of their inability to see the connection between what they really see and what they are willing to believe.

III. He Refused to Forsake Us so He was Forsaken by God (33-36).

A. Nature seemed to know that its Creator was being forsaken. Darkness from noon until 3:00 p.m. in the spring of the year?

B. Jesus seemed to know He was being forsaken. In a great hour of trial He quoted the Bible for strength and perspective. The old gospel preachers would say that God turned His back on His own Son.

C. The bystanders do not seem to know what is going on. They wrongly assume that Jesus is calling for Elijah, when He really is quoting the Bible.

IV. He Refused to Live so we Could Believe and Live Forever (37-39).

A. He really died. Think of it—the Son of God died. Albert Camus said, "People are never convinced of what you believe until you die." The loud cry was a victory shout that John 19:30 records, "It is finished." Even the temple seemed to be aware of the significance of that.

B. He really was God's Son. At least the centurion confessed this. This Gospel had begun, "The beginning of the gospel about Jesus Christ, the Son of God." Now to a Roman audience, a centurion gives the classic confession.

Conclusion

More than an innocent man died that day. God was turning a new page in the history books. Eternal realities were taking place in the real world above us.

Moving Out of the Cemetery

Matthew 28:1-10

Introduction

Easter is scary! If God's Son is really alive then I will have to deal with Him. I have no choice.

I have friends who lived for awhile in the caretaker's house in a cemetery. They were able to live there provided they did some upkeep for the cemetery. They finally found a house to purchase in the town in which they were living. They told a co-worker of mine to be sure to tell me that they would be moving, and, *it's not everyday someone moves out of a cemetery*. That's true, but I know someone who did. And because He did, I shall.

Hear what the angels said as Jesus moved out of the cemetery:

I. Do Not Be Afraid (v. 5).

A. This is the repeated statement of deity and/or angels when they come into the presence of people. Rightly so—sinful man should be afraid when God comes near.

B. But Scripture consistently teaches that we do not need to be afraid. In fact, a word study on "fear" will reveal that there is only one we are to fear, i.e. God. We are told to "not" fear several things, but we are to fear God.

C. We can appreciate why those first women would be afraid. All kind of unnatural things had taken place. Earthquakes, angels sitting on stones, and resurrected people walking around are far from normal. Easter turns the world upside down, but the gracious response of God is, "Don't be afraid."

II. Come and See (v. 6).

A. This is clearly an invitation to our minds by the angels. The God of the Bible respects our intellectual capacity. He is not interested in blind faith. Our future cannot be based on some naive notion that He "might" be alive.

B. Maybe that is why the evidence is so strong. Jesus appears some 13 times, and one of these was to a group of about 500. He did this over a period of 40 days. All theories to explain this away are as unconvincing as the reports of the bribed guard's lie about the body being stolen (28:11-15).

III. Go and Tell (v. 7, 10).

A. Both the angels and Jesus Himself make this request. If Jesus really is alive then the whole world should know. This is what gives substance to the great commission in the latter part of the chapter.

B. The resurrection enlarged Jesus' authority. Out of that authority comes the command to go, disciple, baptize, and teach. In it all He promises His presence through the Holy Spirit.

Conclusion

Many things help explain the missionary efforts of the first century A.D. church. The power of the Holy Spirit, the commitment of those faithful disciples, the hope of heaven, etc. But knowing that Jesus was alive no doubt propelled the church out into the Roman Empire. The early Christians really believed that they had the answer to the problem of cemeteries.

Illustrations

This story could change your life forever. My parents took me to the Passion Play in the Black Hills when I was a very young boy. I remembered it vividly. I wanted my children to have that opportunity. So in the mid 1980's I took my family there. While we waited for the play to begin I did something as an adult that I would never do as a child—I read the program. What I read shocked me. The man who played Jesus Christ when I was a child visiting the play would be the same one to play it that night when I was there with my children. He was in his 80's and was the only one to have ever played the part since bringing the play to the U. S. from Germany in 1938. I was impressed to say the least. When the play was over my wife and I compared notes as to what we liked best. We were in concert. We were so moved by the announcement before the play began by the man's wife who played the angel at the empty tomb. She came on to the stage and a floodlight engulfed her in her angelic garb. She held out her arms horizontally. Her shadow created the picture of a cross. She invited the audience to watch the play carefully. She said, "If you do, this play could change your life forever." It still does.

Sources Cited

Barclay, William. *The Gospel of John*. Volume 2. (Philadelphia: Westminster Press, 1955).

Blomberg, Craig L. *The New American Commentary: Matthew*. (Nashville: Broadman, 1992).

Briscoe, Stuart. "The Meaning of Discipleship." <u>Preaching Today</u>. Tape # 4.

Craddock, Fred B. "The Nod of Recognition" and "The Shock of Recognition." <u>Preaching Today</u>. Tapes # 92 and 93.

Farra, Harry. The Sermon Doctor. Grand Rapids: Baker, 1989.

Cordon, Clarence. *The Cotton Patch Version*. (Clinton, New Jersey: New Win Publishing, Inc, 1968).

Morse, Eugene. *Exodus to a Hidden Valley*. (Cleveland: Collins World, 1974).

Wilson, Seth. *Learning From Jesus*. (Joplin, Missouri: College Press, 1977).